ASTERIX
THE GLADIATOR

TEXT BY GOSCINNY

DRAWINGS BY UDERZO

TRANSLATED BY ANTHEA BELL AND DEREK HOCKRIDGE

DARGAUD PUBLISHING INTERNATIONAL, LTD.

2 Lafayette Court, Greenwich, Connecticut 06830 U.S.A.

ASTERIX THROUGHOUT THE WORLD

AUSTRALIA
Hodder Dargaud, 2 Apollo Place, Lane Cover, New South Wales 2066, Australia

AUSTRIA
Delta Verlag, Postfach 1215, 7000 Stuttgart 1, Federal German Republic

BELGIUM
Dargaud Benelux, 3 rue Kindermans, 1050 Brussels, Belgium

BRAZIL
Record Distribuidora, Rua Argentina 171, 20921 Rio de Janeiro, Brazil

DENMARK
Serieforlaget A/S (Gutenberghus Group), Vognmagergade 11, 1148 Copenhagen K, Denmark

ESPERANTO
Delta Verlag, Postfach 1215, 7 Stuttgart 1, Federal German Republic

FEDERAL GERMAN REPUBLIC
Delta Verlag, Postfach 1215, 7 Stuttgart 1, Federal German Republic

FINLAND
Sanoma Osakeyhtio, Ludviginkatu 2-10, 00130 HELSINKI 13, Finland

FRANCE
Dargaud Editeur, 12 rue Blaise Pascal, 92200 Neuilly sur Seine, France

HOLLAND
Dargaud Benelux, 3 rue Kindermans, 1050 Brussels, Belgium
Distribution : Van Ditmar b.v., Oostelijke Handelskade 11, 1019 BL Amsterdam, Holland

HONG KONG
Hodder Dargaud, c/o United Publishers Book Services, Stanhope House, 7th floor,
734 King's Road, Hong Kong

HUNGARY
Nip Forum, Vojvode Misica 1-3, 2100 Novi Sad, Yugoslavia

INDIA
Gowarsons Publishers Private Ltd., Gulab House, Mayapuri, New Delhi 110 064, India

INDONESIA
Penerbit Sinar Harapan, J1. Dewi Sartika 136 D, POB 015 JNG, Jakarta Indonesia

ISRAEL
Dahlia Pelled Publishers, 5 Hamekoubalim Street, Herzeliah 46447, Israel

ITALY
Bonelli-Dargaud, Via M. Buonarroti 38, 20145 Milan, Italy

NEW ZEALAND
Hodder Dargaud, POB 3858, Auckland 1, New Zealand

NORWAY
A/S Hjemmet (Gutenberghus Group), Kristian den 4 des Gate 13, Oslo 1, Norway

PORTUGAL
Meriberica, Av. Pedro Alvares Cabral 84-1º Dto., 1296 Lisbon Codex, Portugal

ROMAN EMPIRE (Latin)
Delta Verlag, Postfach 1215, 7000 Stuttgart 1, Federal German Republic

SOUTH AFRICA
Hodder Dargaud, PO Box 32213, Braamfontein Centre, Braamfontein 2017,
Johannesburg, South Africa

SOUTH AMERICA
Grijalbo-Dargaud S.A., Deu y Mata 98-102, Barcelona 29, Spain

SPAIN
Grijalbo-Dargaud S.A., Deu y Mata 98-102, Barcelona 29, Spain

SWENDEN
Hemmets Journal Forlag (Gutenberghus Group), Fack 200 22 Malmö, Sweden

SWITZERLAND
Interpress Dargaud S.A., En Budron B, 1052 Le Mont/Lausanne, Switzerland

TURKEY
Kervan Kitabcilik, Basin Sanayii ve Ticaret AS, Tercuman Tesisleri, Topkapi-Istanbul, Turkey

UNITED KINGDOM
Hodder Dargaud, Mill Road, Dunton Green, Sevenoaks, Kent, TN13 2YJ, England

UNITED STATES OF AMERICA & CANADA
Dargaud Publishing International, Ltd., 2 Lafayette Court, Greenwich, Connecticut 06830, U.S.A.

WALES
Gwasg Y Dref Wen, 28 Church Road, Whitchurch, Cardiff, Wales

YUGOSLAVIA
Nip Forum, Vojvode Misica 1-3, 2100 Novi Sad, Yugoslavia

Printed in Italy by Fratelli Pagano (Genoa)

Exclusive Licenced Distributor
DARGAUD PUBLISHING INTERNATIONAL. LTD
2 Lafayette Court, Greenwich, Connecticut 06830, U.S.A.

GAULISH VILLAGE

COMPENDIUM

LAUDANUM

AQUARIUM

TOTORUM

A R M O R I C A

BELGICA

LUTETIA

GAUL
(ROMAN CONQUEST)
50 B.C.

C E L T I C A

P R O V I N C I A

A Q U I T A N I A

The year is 50 BC. Gaul is entirely occupied by the Romans. Well, not entirely… One small village of indomitable Gauls still holds out against the invaders. And life is not easy for the Roman legionaries who garrison the fortified camps of Totorum, Aquarium, Laudanum and Compendium…

a few of the Gauls

Asterix, the hero of these adventures. A shrewd, cunning little warrior; all perilous missions are immediately entrusted to him. Asterix gets his superhuman strength from the magic potion brewed by the druid Getafix...

Obelix, Asterix's inseparable friend. A menhir delivery-man by trade; addicted to wild boar. Obelix is always ready to drop everything and go off on a new adventure with Asterix — so long as there's wild boar to eat, and plenty of fighting.

Getafix, the venerable village druid. Gathers mistletoe and brews magic potions. His speciality is the potion which gives the drinker superhuman strength. But Getafix also has other recipes up his sleeve...

Cacofonix, the bard. Opinion is divided as to his musical gifts. Cacofonix thinks he's a genius. Everyone else thinks he's unspeakable. But so long as he doesn't speak, let alone sing, everybody likes him...

Finally, Vitalstatistix, the chief of the tribe. Majestic, brave and hot-tempered, the old warrior is respected by his men and feared by his enemies. Vitalstatistix himself has only one fear; he is afraid the sky may fall on his head tomorrow. But as he always says, 'Tomorrow never comes.'

THE ROMAN CAMP OF COMPENDIUM IS IN A FERMENT. THE PREFECT OF GAUL, ODIUS ASPARAGUS, IS PAYING A CALL ON CENTURION GRACCHUS ARMISURPLUS. THE PREFECT ARRIVES FROM THE NEARBY COAST WHERE HIS GALLEY HAS PUT IN...

PRESENT... PILUM!...

AVE, PREFECT! THIS IS A GREAT HONOUR FOR ME!

AVE, CENTURION! YOU'RE TELLING ME!

AND NOW FOR THE PURPOSE OF MY VISIT, CENTURION! I'M GOING TO ROME ON LEAVE, AND CUSTOM DECREES THAT I TAKE CAESAR A HANDSOME PRESENT... SOMETHING UNUSUAL AND VERY VALUABLE...

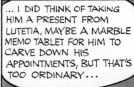

... I DID THINK OF TAKING HIM A PRESENT FROM LUTETIA, MAYBE A MARBLE MEMO TABLET FOR HIM TO CARVE DOWN HIS APPOINTMENTS, BUT THAT'S TOO ORDINARY...

THEN I HAD A BRILLIANT IDEA! WHY NOT TAKE CAESAR ONE OF THE INVINCIBLE GAULS FROM HEREABOUTS?

WHAT?!

BUT, PREFECT, ABOUT THESE INVINCIBLE GAULS ... THERE'S JUST ONE SNAG!

WELL, WHAT IS IT?

THEY HAPPEN TO BE INVINCIBLE!

THAT'S WHAT MAKES THEM SO VALUABLE! GET ME ONE OF THESE GAULS, AND YOU WON'T REGRET IT!

THERE'S CERTAINLY ONE WHO'S A BIT MORE HARMLESS THAN THE OTHERS... CACOFONIX THE BARD. HE OFTEN GOES FOR WALKS IN THE FOREST BY HIMSELF LOOKING FOR INSPIRATION!

EXCELLENT! I MUST HAVE THIS BARD—AND FAST!

AND IN THE GAULISH VILLAGE...

GOODBYE, ASTERIX, I'M GOING FOR A WALK IN THE FOREST!

GOODBYE, CACOFONIX!

THE BATTLE IS SHORT...

CLINKCLANKCLONK!

BANG!

BIFF!

BUT SHARP...

SWOOOSH!

I CAN'T FIND CACOFONIX ANYWHERE... AH, THERE'S THE ROMAN COMMANDER!

BANG!

BING!

I SHALL FIGHT TO THE DEATH!

WANT ME TO THUMP YOU?

OH ALL RIGHT! ALL IS LOST! I SURRENDER! ALEA JACTA EST!

AND LET IT BE A LESSON TO YOU! NOW, GIVE US BACK OUR BARD, AND DON'T DO IT AGAIN!

THE FACT IS... YOUR BARD ISN'T HERE ANY MORE. AT THIS MOMENT HE'S ON BOARD A GALLEY, SAILING FOR ROME TO BE GIVEN TO CAESAR AS A PRESENT...

!!!

WE'RE WASTING OUR TIME...

A PRESENT? THAT'S A REALLY FUNNY IDEA!

LOOK AT THIS, ASTERIX! I'M SURE I'VE WON OUR BET! AND ONE LEGIONARY WAS FIGHTING BARE-HEADED TOO. IT'S AGAINST ALL THE RULES OF WARFARE TO GO INTO BATTLE IMPROPERLY DRESSED! I'VE A GOOD MIND TO REPORT HIM!

THE GAULS WITHDRAW, LEAVING BEHIND THEM THE AFTERMATH OF BATTLE...

THEY REALLY LET US HAVE IT, EH, SIR?

IN THE FIRST PLACE, GET THIS CAMP BACK INTO ORDER!!! WHAT'S ALL THIS UNTIDINESS IN AID OF? AND DON'T ANYONE EVER MENTION THIS BATTLE TO ME AGAIN!!!

WELL, SO WE'VE GOT A DATE AT INSTANTMIX'S PLACE THIS EVENING. WHAT DO WE DO TILL THEN?

WE COULD GO BACK AND HAVE SOME MORE BOAR?

BOAR ON THE SPIT

THE BATHS! I'VE OFTEN HEARD ABOUT THE ROMAN BATHS! LET'S GO AND HAVE A BATH!

THERMAE

GO AND GET UNDRESSED IN THE APODYTERIA

THAT MUST MEAN THE CHANGING ROOM...

THIS WAY, NOBLE LORDS!

IS IT US HE MEANS?

APODYTERIA

WE HAVEN'T GOT MUCH ON. I HOPE WE DON'T CATCH COLD!

SVDATORIA

IT'S HOT IN HERE!

I WONDER IF WE COULD OPEN A WINDOW

LOOK, CAIUS FATUOUS! YOU'RE ALWAYS ON THE LOOKOUT FOR GLADIATORS — WHAT DO YOU THINK OF THOSE TWO MEN?

INTERESTING. ESPECIALLY THE FAT ONE

CALDARIVM

LET'S TRY IN HERE... IT MAY BE COOLER

THIS WAS A FUNNY IDEA OF YOURS, ASTERIX, BY TOUTATIS!

HE SAID, 'BY TOUTATIS'... THEY'RE GAULS...

WE MAY BE HARD-BOILED, BUT THIS IS OVERDOING IT!

YOU SEEM TO BE STRANGERS HERE. I'LL GUIDE YOU ROUND THE BATHS. I COME HERE REGULARLY FOR MY HEALTH, THOUGH IT IS A BIT OF A SWEAT...

YOU SHOULD GO TO THE FRIGIDARIUM AND DIVE INTO THE POOL OF ICY WATER

ICY WATER? I'M ON MY WAY!

WATCH ME DIVE, ASTERIX! WATCH ME DIVE!

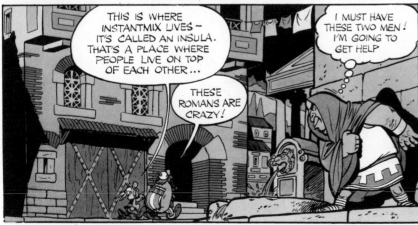

YES, I DID HEAR ABOUT THE BARD THAT THE PREFECT OF GAUL GAVE CAESAR AS A PRESENT...

IT SEEMS THAT THIS BARD IS TO BE THROWN TO THE LIONS AT THE NEXT GAMES IN THE CIRCUS MAXIMUS, IN A FEW DAYS' TIME...

!!

WE'LL RESCUE HIM!

YOU CAN'T. THE BARD'S BEEN SHUT UP IN A CELL IN THE CIRCUS...AND IT'S A MAXIMUM SECURITY CIRCUS!

BANG!

BUT THERE'S WORSE TO COME. THAT'S WHY I WARNED YOU TO BE CAREFUL. YOU MUST BE INDOMITABLE GAULS LIKE THE BARD! YOU MUST FLEE FROM ROME!

CAIUS FATUOUS, WHO TRAINS THE GLADIATORS, IS LOOKING FOR MEN FOR THE GAMES... AND INDOMITABLE GAULS ARE IN GREAT DEMAND!

WE WILL RESCUE OUR BARD!

YOU ACT THE FINE LADY AND YOU CAN'T EVEN AFFORD A SLAVE TO DO THE HOUSEWORK!

SO I AM A FINE LADY! SO YOU KNOW WHAT THE FINE LADY HAS TO SAY TO YOU?

BY JUNO, IF YOU DON'T SHUT UP I'M CALLING THE WATCH!

THESE ROMANS ARE CRAZY!

THERE THEY ARE!

WE'RE BEING ATTACKED!

GOODY!

LOOK, ASTERIX! I'VE THOUGHT OF SOMETHING NEW! LOOK, I DON'T EVEN TOUCH THEM, I SHAKE THEM! IT LASTS LONGER THAT WAY!

ALL RIGHT, OBELIX. PUT HIM DOWN NOW!

WILL YOU BE QUIET OUT THERE IN THE ROAD! WE CAN'T HEAR OURSELVES SHOUT IN HERE!

19

THIS INN OPPOSITE THE CIRCUS WILL SUIT US NICELY. LET'S SEE IF THEY HAVE ANY ROOM

RIGHT

CIRCUS INN

I WONDER IF THEY'LL LET US IN AT THIS TIME OF NIGHT...

I'LL JUST KNOCK...

SOON AFTERWARDS...

THAT WILL BE 20 SESTERTII FOR THE NIGHT AND 40 SESTERTII FOR THE DOOR

TAP! TAP! TAP!

MEANWHILE IN THE HOUSE OF CAIUS FATUOUS THE GLADIATOR TRAINER...

WELL, DID YOU GET THEM?

ER... NO, BOSS... THEY DIDN'T WANT TO COME

I MUST HAVE THOSE TWO MEN! JUMP TO IT, EVERY-ONE!

AND NEXT MORNING...

SLEEP WELL, ASTERIX?

YES, THANK YOU, OBELIX. LET'S GO AND HAVE BREAKFAST NOW

WE MUST TRY TO GET INTO CONVERSATION WITH ONE OF THE CIRCUS GUARDS AND FIND OUT EXACTLY WHERE CACOFONIX IS IMPRISONED!

WAITER! HAVE YOU BY ANY CHANCE GOT SOME PARSLEY?

PARSLEY? WHAT FOR?

FOR PUTTING IN MY EARS! I'VE GOT A PRISONER WHO KEEPS ON SINGING, SOMETHING HORRIBLE!

THAT'S CACOFONIX!

THE DESCRIPTION FITS, ANYWAY!

20

24

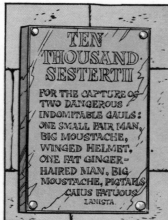

TIME PASSES BY, AND THE GLADIATORS ARE PUTTING ON WEIGHT...

MY FIRST IS A HUNDRED, MY SECOND IS A SIGN OF THE ZODIAC, MY THIRD IS A HIBERNIAN, MY FOURTH IS THE EGYPTIAN GOD OF THE SUN AND JULIUS CAESAR LOVES MY WHOLE! WHO AM I?

WHILE CAIUS FATUOUS IS LOSING IT...

THERE THEY GO AGAIN! PLAYING IDIOTIC GAMES INSTEAD OF TRAINING! A FINE CIRCUS THIS IS GOING TO BE!

IT'S C, LEO, PAT, RA... CLEOPATRA!

THAT WAS A DIFFICULT ONE THAT WAS!

THE GAMES ARE FIXED FOR TOMORROW. THIS WILL BE YOUR LAST NIGHT IN THE CIRCUS, YOU USELESS LOT!

WE DON'T REALLY WANT TO FIGHT ANY MORE, ASTERIX

DON'T WORRY! I PROMISE YOU WON'T HAVE TO RISK YOUR LIVES IN THE ARENA!

AND A VERY RELAXED GROUP OF GLADIATORS ARRIVES AT THE CIRCUS...

HA, HA! HO, HO!

STOP PUSHING, WILL YOU!

PORPUS IS A BEAST! PASS IT ON!

WHAT'S THE MATTER WITH THEM?

NO IDEA. LOCK THEM UP DOWN BELOW!

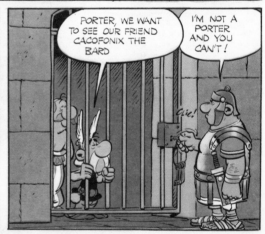

PORTER, WE WANT TO SEE OUR FRIEND CACOFONIX THE BARD

I'M NOT A PORTER AND YOU CAN'T!

VERY WELL THEN, WE SHALL TEAR OUT THESE BARS ONE BY ONE UNTIL YOU CO-OPERATE!

GO AHEAD AND TRY!

PLINNNK!

PLONNNK!

PLUNNNK!

STOP! LEAVE THE FIXTURES ALONE!

AH, ABOUT TIME TOO! WHAT SERVICE!

A HUGE CROWD IS FORMING OUTSIDE THE CIRCUS...

WASH YOUR TOGAS IN SUPER PERSIC! SUPER PERSIC WASHES EVEN PURPLER!

SCORE CARD! SCORE CARD!

CUSHIONS! CUSHIONS!

CHIPOLATAE! CANES CALIDI! CHIPOLATAE!

AND INSIDE THE IMPOSING ARENA THE TRUMPETS ANNOUNCE THE ARRIVAL OF CAESAR IN THE IMPERIAL BOX...

TANTAN TARA!!!!

PANEM ET CIRCENSES

LONG LIVE CAESAR!

CAESAR FOR EVER!

EVERYONE APPLAUDS THE DICTATOR...

CLAP! CLAP! CLAP! CLAP! CLAP! CLAP!

ET TU BRUTE!

CLAP! CLAP! CLAP!

*YOU TOO, BRUTUS!

THAT BRUTUS...I CAN SEE I'M GOING TO HAVE TROUBLE WITH HIM*

CLAPCLAP! CLAPCLAP! CLAPCLAP! CLAPCLAP!

*AN EXAMINATION OF ACT III, SCENE 1 OF JULIUS CAESAR BY WILLIAM SHAKESPEARE WILL INDICATE THE PROPHETIC NATURE OF THIS REMARK

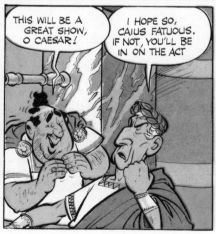

THIS WILL BE A GREAT SHOW, O CAESAR!

I HOPE SO, CAIUS FATUOUS. IF NOT, YOU'LL BE IN ON THE ACT

LET THE GAMES BEGIN!

GULP!

38

43

... AND FINALLY I ASK YOU TO FREE THE GLADIATORS. THEY'RE GIVING UP THEIR BLOODTHIRSTY JOB!

GRANTED, O GAUL!

MMPH? IS THE SHOW OVER YET?

I ASK YOU TO FREE THE BARD WE CAME TO RESCUE, AND LET US GO HOME TO GAUL BEFORE WE HAVE TO BEAT YOUR ARMY UP AGAIN...

AND I HAVE ONE LAST FAVOUR TO ASK YOU, JULIUS...

YOU SAW THAT? NOT A BAD PROGRAMME, EH?

LEND US CAIUS FATUOUS THE GLADIATOR TRAINER FOR OUR JOURNEY BACK TO GAUL. WE'LL SEND HIM BACK BY RETURN

GRANTED, BY JUPITER!

BUT... BUT...

WHAT ARE YOU GOING TO DO WITH ME?

WE'RE GOING TO TEACH YOU A LITTLE LESSON, BY BELENOS!

LONG LIVE THE GAULS!

LONG LIVE THE GLADIATORS!

LONG LIVE CAESAR!

WHAT HAPPENED TO ME?

EXACTLY WHAT WILL HAPPEN AGAIN IF YOU DARE SING A NOTE BEFORE WE GET BACK TO GAUL!

NO FEAR! I'M NOT SINGING FOR ANY MORE ROMAN BARBARIANS, AND MOREOVER I'M TAKING NO FURTHER INTEREST IN THE MATTER!

HEY, WHERE ARE THE RUINS? DIDN'T A HOUSE FALL ON ME?

42

AND AFTER A FEW HOURS' WALK...

O EKONOMIKRISIS, PHOENICIAN MERCHANT, WILL YOU KEEP YOUR PROMISE AND TAKE US BACK TO GAUL?

MY OLD FRIENDS THE GAULS!!!

COME ABOARD, FRIENDS! BUSINESS WAS GOOD. I HAVE SOLD EVERYTHING, AND NOW I HAVE TO STOCK UP AGAIN!

WHO'S THIS?

A LITTLE SURPRISE FOR YOUR ROWING PARTNERS!

DO I...DO I HAVE TO ROW ALL BY MYSELF? ALL THE WAY BACK TO GAUL?

THIS WILL TEACH YOU TO DO A DIRTY JOB AND LIVE OFF OTHER PEOPLE'S MUSCLE!

WHY DON'T I SING A LITTLE SOMETHING TO LIVEN HIM UP?

NOOOO!

HE'S GREAT!

WHAT AN OARSMAN!

HEAR, HEAR!

SPLAT, SPLAT, SPAT, SPLAT, SPLAT, SPLAT

I FEEL WE MIGHT MAKE THIS ROMAN A PARTNER!

AN EXCELLENT NOTION, MR. CHAIRMAN!

BAH!

THE VOYAGE IS UNEVENTFUL, EXCEPT FOR A SKIRMISH WITH THE PIRATES...

WE SURE UNLUCKY WID DEM GAULS, SAH!

43

the end